MW00903574

The BIRTH of JESUS

Elizabeth Dolezal

xulon
PRESS

Merry Christmas, Jackson, Emery & Taylor!
Immanuel!)
♡Elizabeth Dolezal
2017

The Birth of Jesus
by Elizabeth Dolezal

Printed in the United States of America.

ISBN 9781629529264

Request information: emdolez@gmail.com
Story, photos, and figures by Elizabeth Dolezal.
Edited by Julie Klusty, jfklusty@gmail.com

www.xulonpress.com

This book is dedicated to my children.

It is a gift to be your mother.
Jesus loves you.

Many years ago, a virgin woman named Mary lived in Nazareth, a town in Galilee. Mary was engaged to marry a man named Joseph.

God sent an angel named Gabriel to
Mary with a message.

Gabriel said to her, "Greetings, Mary! The Lord is
with you. You are very special to Him!"

Mary was frightened, but the angel said,
"Do not be afraid, Mary. You have found favor
with God. You will give birth to a son,
whom you will name Jesus.
He will be the Son of God."

Mary was found to be with child before she and Joseph came together as man and wife. Joseph considered leaving Mary.

After Joseph considered this, an angel of the Lord appeared to him in a dream and said, "Joseph, do not be afraid to take Mary as your wife. The baby she is carrying is from the Holy Spirit.

She will give birth to a son, and you are to give Him the name Jesus. He will be called Immanuel, meaning 'God is with us.' He will save His people from their sins."

When Joseph woke up, he obeyed the angel of the Lord and took Mary home as his wife.

Soon after, King Caesar Augustus commanded that a census be taken of the entire Roman kingdom, and everyone was ordered to return to their hometown to be counted.

Joseph was a descendant of David, so he and Mary traveled many miles to Bethlehem, the town of David, in Judea. Mary rode on a donkey. Joseph walked.

When they arrived in Bethlehem, it was very crowded with people who were there for the census. All of the inns were full, and there was no room for them to sleep. One friendly innkeeper took pity on them when he saw that Mary was pregnant. He said they could stay in his stable, where he kept his ox.

Joseph made a bed of hay for Mary, and they lay down to sleep.

During the night, the time came for the baby to be born. Mary gave birth in the stable with the ox and donkey looking on. They named the baby Jesus. Mary held Him in her arms and was filled with love and joy.

Mary wrapped Him in a soft blanket and laid
Him in a manger filled with fresh hay.

In a field nearby, there were shepherds watching over their flocks of sheep. Suddenly, an angel of the Lord appeared to them, surrounded by bright light. The shepherds were very frightened.

The angel said, "Do not be afraid. I have good news of great joy for people all over the world. Today, in Bethlehem, the Savior has been born. He is Christ the Lord."

The angel told the shepherds they would find the baby wrapped in a blanket and lying in a manger.

Suddenly, more heavenly angels appeared! They praised God, singing, "Glory to God in the highest. On earth, peace and good will toward men."

When the angels returned to heaven, the shepherds looked at each other and said, "Let us go to Bethlehem to look for the Savior the angels told us about."

The shepherds hurried to
Bethlehem with their sheep.

They found Mary, Joseph, and baby Jesus, who was lying in the manger just as the angel had said. They knelt down and worshipped baby Jesus. Later, they told everyone who would listen to them the amazing things they had seen and heard.

Mary often thought about that night.

A new star appeared in the sky, signifying the birth of Jesus in Bethlehem. Wise men saw the star and knew that a king had been born.

They said to each other, "Let us follow the star and bring gifts to the new King."

They set off on their long journey, and the star guided them. The wise men followed the star because they wanted to worship the baby who was born King of the Jews.

The wise men continued to follow the star as it went ahead of them for many miles, until it stopped over the place where the child Jesus was living. When they saw that the star had stopped, they were overjoyed.

When they arrived at the house that the star shone on, they saw the child Jesus with His mother, Mary. They bowed down and worshiped Him. Then they gave Him gifts of frankincense, gold, and myrrh.

Jesus Christ, our Savior, was sent to us by God.
He was born in Bethlehem to the Virgin Mary.
We celebrate His birth on Christmas Day!

If you would like to create your own crocheted Nativity Scene, like the one featured in this book, patterns are available for purchase at https://www.etsy.com.

Search for Complete
Nativity Scene Crochet Pattern
by Elizabeth Dolezal in the
ElizabethMDolezal shop.

The idea for the crocheted Nativity Scene featured in this book came from the author's lovely daughter, Ayvee. Eagerly awaiting the completion of each piece, Ayvee inspired her mom to be creative while designing the set.

The special heirloom will be enjoyed by the family for many Christmases to come.